MYTHS AND MISCONCEPTIONS

Uncovering the Truth about
Napoleon's Height,
Lemmings, the Space Pen,
the Salem Witch Trials, and Other
Things You Thought You Knew

Richard Benson

RACEHORSE PUBLISHING

MYTHS AND MISCONCEPTIONS

Racehorse Publishing books may be purchased in bulk at special discounts for sales promotion, corporate gifts, fund-raising, or educational purposes. Special editions can also be created to specifications. For details, contact the Special Sales Department, Skyhorse Publishing, 307 West 36th Street, 11th Floor, New York, NY 10018 or info@skyhorsepublishing.com.

Racehorse Publishing™ is a pending trademark of Skyhorse Publishing, Inc.®, a Delaware corporation.

Visit our website at www.skyhorsepublishing.com.

10 9 8 7 6 5 4 3 2 1

Library of Congress Cataloging-in-Publication Data is available on file.

ISBN: 978-1-63158-408-4
E-Book ISBN: 978-1-63158-416-9

Printed in China

I am suspicious of all the things
that the average citizen believes.

H. L. Mencken

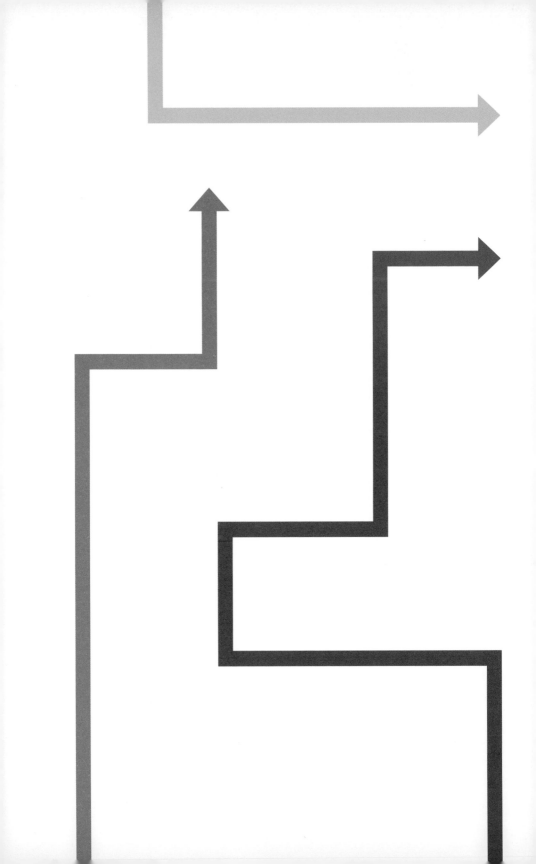

INTRODUCTION

Do you believe everything other people tell you? Well, perhaps it's time to start questioning things a little more closely, for many of the things most people think are true are actually complete misconceptions. Say something often enough, though, and it will be accepted as the truth. We are bombarded with so much information that we often take things for granted, because it's easier to do that than it is to find out the facts behind the fiction. In some cases, people prefer the "faux" facts, even though they know they are wrong, thus perpetuating stubborn fallacies that just won't go away.

Did you know, for example, that Jerusalem artichokes do not come from Jerusalem, or that Columbus did not discover America? You can find the truth behind these original "fake news" stories and many others in the pages that follow. The entries are not in any particular order, so you can open the book anywhere at random to discover the surprises within.

St. Bernards do not carry brandy kegs. Everyone knows St. Bernard dogs carry barrels of brandy around their necks to help stranded travelers they have been sent to rescue in the Alps. But, sadly, it's not actually true (and brandy wouldn't help anyone who had been caught in an avalanche in any event—see the next entry). The myth about St. Bernards can be attributed to the brilliant painter Edwin Landseer who, at the age of just 17, produced a picture of two rescue dogs, one of which, for artistic effect, was depicted with a keg on its collar.

Alcohol does not warm you. It is generally believed that drinking alcohol warms the body. In fact, it simply causes warm blood to move closer to the skin, making it feel warmer while the rest of the body cools down. But don't tell anyone else the truth about this—it gives you a good excuse whenever you fancy a snifter.

THE MYTH

NASA spent millions developing a "space pen."

THE TRUTH

During the space race in the 1960s, astronauts needed a different way to write things down, since regular pens don't work without gravity. The story goes that NASA spent years working on a special gravity-defying pen, at great expense to the American taxpayer, while the more shrewd Russian cosmonauts simply used a pencil. However, there are multiple elements of this story that aren't true: both astronauts and cosmonauts originally used pencils (though their flammable qualities and the fact that broken bits of graphite could float into delicate machinery made them less than ideal), and it was the work and money of a separate company (the Fisher Pen Company) that finally came up with the "space pen" that replaced pencils.

Queen Victoria never said, "We are not amused." There is no evidence that this was said by Queen Victoria, although it is frequently quoted. Perhaps she would now not be amused by the lack of evidence that she did or did not say it.

Panama hats don't come from Panama. The Panama hat, woven with the plaited leaves of a palm-like plant, originated in Ecuador, where it is still made. The name arose when Ecuadorian hat makers took their trade to Panama to benefit from the thriving tourist market there, and when people referred to the hats they had bought in Panama the name stuck.

There is more caffeine in a regular coffee than in a single shot of espresso. While espresso does have a higher concentration of caffeine, the overall amount is offset by its tiny size in comparison to a standard cup of brewed coffee.

You can't detox your body. The idea that you can "flush" or "cleanse" your body of toxins through juices, teas, diets, and special pills is a scam with absolutely no basis in science. If your body wasn't capable of getting rid of those toxins on its own (hey, that's your kidneys, liver, and lungs' job!), you would probably be dead. So put down that weird herbal detox tea and rest safe in the knowledge that a healthy body will be doing all the detoxing you'll ever need.

Coffee is not made from beans. Chocolate-coated coffee beans are delicious, right? Except that in saying this you would actually be wrong, for what most people think of as coffee beans are not beans at all—they are seeds. But at least they still taste great, whatever they're called, so you can leave the terminology to the botanists and get on with enjoying your delicious "beans."

THE MYTH

Lemmings commit suicide
by jumping off cliffs.

THE TRUTH

The claim that lemmings are suicidal and dive off cliff-edges en masse has been around since at least the nineteenth century, but was never based on fact. The idea was perpetuated in the twentieth century by the Disney film *White Wilderness*, which staged migration scenes using multiple shots of relatively small groups of lemmings dropping off cliffs into the water below in order to swim to the other side of the body of water in question (in this instance, it turned out to be the Arctic Sea, so there was no other side and the lemmings would all have drowned, but not deliberately). The filmmakers even pushed some lemmings off the cliff to get certain bits of footage.

Medieval Europeans did not believe the earth is flat. Pythagoras, Aristotle, and other Ancient Greek polymaths had provided a body of empirical evidence that the earth is spherical by around 330 BCE, and belief in a spherical earth was almost universal among intellectuals from that time onwards.

The Bayeux Tapestry is not a tapestry. Although known as the "Bayeux Tapestry," this amazing work of art is actually an embroidery. A tapestry is woven on a loom, whereas an embroidery consists of threads sewn on to a ground fabric to create a picture.

Frankenstein isn't the name of Mary Shelley's monster. In Shelley's novel *Frankenstein; or, The Modern Prometheus*, Victor Frankenstein is the name of the creature's creator. The monster itself is not named.

Vinegar does not stop you from crying when chopping onions. There are various suggestions for stopping your eyes watering when cutting onions, including lighting a candle, having a fan on nearby, holding a piece of bread in your mouth, microwaving or freezing the onion prior to chopping, and covering the chopping board with vinegar. However, none of these have been scientifically proven to work.

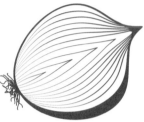

Cranberry juice is not an effective cure or prevention for urinary tract infections (UTIs). Long-held advice has it that the acidity of cranberry juice creates a hostile environment for germs in the urinary tract, thereby killing off infections. Sadly, this is all just wishful thinking, as studies have shown that you would have to consume an impractically large quantity of cranberry juice for it to have any effect. (What a pleasant medical treatment it would be, though!) You're better off just drinking water.

THE MYTH

Lightning never strikes the same place twice.

THE TRUTH

There are well-documented accounts of lightning striking the same place more than once. In fact, it is almost inevitable that some places will get hit several times, with tall structures the most likely to be hit repeatedly. In everyday use, the associated phrase "lightning never strikes twice in the same place" (meaning it is unlikely that something untoward will happen more than once) may offer some comfort, but it's based on a lie.

Sharks do get cancer. The idea that sharks are somehow immune from cancer is just propaganda spread by those who sell shark cartilage as a miracle "cure" for the disease—scientists have been aware of cancerous cells and tumors in a variety of shark species for hundreds of years.

Humphrey Bogart did not say, "Play it again, Sam." It may be the most quoted line from the 1942 film *Casablanca*—but neither Humphrey Bogart nor Ingrid Bergman ever said it. In fact, Bogart said "Play it" and Bergman added "Play it, Sam," but their lines have been misquoted ever since.

There is not a dark side of the moon. Although frequently referred to as such, the moon does not have a permanently dark side. It rotates on its own axis, meaning half the time the far side is in darkness, while for the other half it's in daylight, just like the earth.

Frozen fruit and vegetables are better for you than fresh ones. Fresh fruit and veggies are normally considered the best way to get your five a day, but the truth is those products have probably been in transit and on display for weeks, rotting and losing nutrients the whole time. Freezing, on the other hand, captures the produce in its prime and retains more vitamins and minerals.

Diamonds are not rare. The truth is that diamonds are actually one of the most commonly found gems on earth. Their "rarity" was originally claimed by the diamond mining and retail group De Beers, which held back large supplies of diamonds to create demand and thus inflate their value.

THE MYTH

Ostriches bury their heads in the sand.

THE TRUTH

Although many people believe this to be true because they have seen photographs that appear to confirm the strange habit, ostriches are not that stupid. They burrow their nests into the ground, so when they put their small heads into the nest to turn their eggs, it looks, from a distance, as if they are putting their heads into the ground. The same thing happens when they eat into the roots of plants. It is just as well that ostriches do not bury their heads in the sand, because they would not be able to breathe if they did, and they would also get sand up their noses.

Lions are not kings of the jungle. Although they are a roaring success, lions do not live in jungles. They roam mainly on the grasslands of East Africa and the scrub-strewn sands of the Kalahari Desert—without a jungle in sight! Somehow, though, "king of the scrublands" doesn't sound quite so impressive, so maybe that's why they got promoted to "kings of the jungle."

Wet hair will not give you a cold. Some people believe that if you go outside with wet hair you will catch a cold, but this isn't true because colds are contracted through a virus, and certainly not because you have damp hair. It's just a hair-raising myth.

Houseflies do not live for only a day. In fact, houseflies can live for up to a month—unless you are handy with a fly swatter.

Not all wood floats. It's generally assumed that if you throw wood into water it will float, which is certainly handy for a game of Poohsticks. Although it's true that most woods will float, however, there are many woods that have a higher density than water and simply will not float for that reason. One such wood is lignum vitae, which is the hardest wood in the world.

Camels do not carry water in their humps. Camels can survive for up to seven months without water. This has led to the belief that water is stored in the camel's hump (or humps, depending on the type of camel), but in fact each hump is filled with fat. Camels have simply evolved to take on and retain vast quantities of water (they can drink up to 20 to 50 gallons of water at a time) to cope with dehydration.

THE MYTH

Vikings wore horned helmets.

THE TRUTH

There is no evidence that Vikings ever wore helmets embellished with horns or large wings as often depicted in books and films. From the seventeenth century onwards, European artists portrayed Vikings with horned helmets, seemingly having got the idea from the horned headdresses that Vikings were described as using for ceremonial purposes (but never in battle) by ancient writers. In 1876, the myth was consolidated by costume designer Carl Emil Doepler, who created horned helmets for Wagner's opera *Der Ring des Nibelungen* (*The Ring of the Nibelung*), probably basing his ideas on pre-Viking German and Scandinavian costumes. The horned helmets do look impressive, though, so who really cares how they came about!

A tomato is not a vegetable. Technically, a tomato is a fruit. Other fruits masquerading as vegetables include cucumbers, avocados, bell peppers, pumpkins, squashes, eggplants, and even zucchinis. Some fruits, including bananas, eggplants, grapes, and tomatoes, are technically also berries, but— to confuse matters even further— strawberries, raspberries, and blackberries aren't.

The Austrian national anthem is not "Edelweiss." Their national anthem is, in fact, *"Land der Berge, Land am Strome"* ("Land of Mountains, Land by the River").

The Romans did not use a "vomitorium" to be sick in. The popular misconception of a vomitorium is that it was where Ancient Romans went to "throw up" during enormous feasts to make room in their stomachs for more food. In actual fact, it was a passageway used to enter or exit an amphitheatre.

The Great Wall of China is not the only man-made object visible from outer space. The Great Wall of China is visible from space only at the lower part of low earth orbit, and only under favorable conditions—not from outer space at all. This is further compounded by the fact that many other man-made objects, including cities, dams, and highways, are also visible from low earth orbit in the right conditions, so it's not a particularly great distinction in any event.

George Washington did not cut down a cherry tree. A popular story has it that a young George Washington damaged his father's beloved cherry tree with a hatchet. His father was said to be initially angry, but George's honesty in confessing to the deed ("I cannot tell a lie, I did cut the tree") reportedly made his father so proud that he let George off the hook. However, the sweet story has no basis in truth and only made an appearance in the fifth edition of Mason Locke Weems' best-selling biography, *The Life of Washington*, to pander to adoring audiences.

THE MYTH

George Washington's false teeth were made of wood.

THE TRUTH

That George Washington had wooden false teeth is a generally accepted fact, but it was never a practical possibility. In fact, he had several sets of false teeth, some made from human teeth (probably purchased from slaves), others made of ivory. He was plagued with poor dental health throughout his adult life, not uncommon at that time, and he tried all sorts of remedies. By the time he became the first President of the United States in 1789, at the age of 57, he only had one good tooth left, so Dr. John Greenwood made him a set of teeth made from hippopotamus and elephant ivory, held together by gold springs. The myth about his false teeth probably arose from the worn, grained appearance his dentures took on over time, which may well have resembled wood.

Walter Hunt did not invent the first safety pin. The invention of the safety pin is generally credited to the American mechanic Walter Hunt in 1849. Although he did secure a patent for the safety pin as it is mass produced today, similar pins were in fact used by the Mycenaeans as long ago as the thirteenth century BCE.

Mary Magdalene was not a prostitute. Mary Magdalene is recorded in the Bible as one of the many followers of Jesus, but there was never any suggestion in the Bible that she was a repentant prostitute. Such rumors only became prevalent in the Middle Ages.

Black holes are not holes. They are enormous, dense areas of space-time mass, which have a gravitational pull so strong that nothing, not even light, can escape from them.

Canute did not try to stop the tide. Canute, or Cnut, King of England and parts of Scandinavia from 1016 to 1035, is much ridiculed for his notorious attempt to stop the tide by setting up his throne on a beach and commanding the incoming sea to stop, with, naturally, embarrassing results. However, the original story, as told by Henry of Huntingdon in the twelfth century, claimed that Canute was actually trying to prove that the power of the gods is far superior to that of humans—even kings. So he expected the result he got, painting him in a far saner light than the later amendment to the story.

Watching TV will not damage your eyes. Parents often claim that too much television permanently damages the eyes, or even makes them "go square," in an attempt to encourage their kids to do their homework or go to bed. Whilst there was an element of danger from some General Electric TV sets in the sixties, which did apparently emit excessive X-rays, modern sets aren't going to cause lasting damage to your eyes.

THE MYTH

Lady Godiva rode naked through Coventry.

THE TRUTH

One English legend claims that Lady Godiva was an eleventh-century noblewoman who rode naked through the streets of Coventry, with only her long hair to cover her modesty, on the proviso that everyone should remain indoors with their windows shut. Later versions of the legend include mention of a tailor, known ever since as Peeping Tom, who ignored the instruction to stay indoors. As a result, he was struck blind or dead, depending upon which version you read. Lady Godiva supposedly made the ride in protest against her husband's oppressive taxation of the populace, but modern historians doubt the veracity of the story as no contemporary record of the event has ever been found—the story didn't in fact appear until the thirteenth century.

Mars is not red. Mars is often described as the "red planet," but it is not red. The apparent color is caused by the high levels of iron found in the dust that covers the planet's surface, which close up actually appears more of a butterscotch color.

Humans and dinosaurs did not co-exist. Just in case you'd been under any illusions thanks to the many films featuring both humans and dinosaurs in the same era, we thought we'd clarify that the two never co-existed. Dinosaurs died out some 65 million years ago, whereas the first human-like creatures didn't appear until around six million years ago.

The earth is not round. From space, the earth appears to be round, but in fact, because it rotates, it is flattened at its poles and slightly swollen around the equator. Technically, the earth is an oblate spheroid—something to excite your guests with next time you have a dinner party!

The word "gringo" didn't originally refer to the US military. "Gringo" is used in Spanish and Portuguese-speaking countries to refer to non-native speakers of their language. Many explanations have been suggested for the origin of the word, including the one that Mexicans or Puerto Ricans shouted "Green go home" when US forces invaded their countries wearing green uniforms in the nineteenth century. The most likely explanation, however, is that the word comes from *griego* (Spanish for "Greek"), which was then extended to include all foreigners.

The Yeti never existed. The existence of the Yeti, or Abominable Snowman, is a popular tale in Himalayan folklore. Sightings of the Yeti or their footprints have been reported for centuries, and some people have even claimed relics relating to the elusive creature. But the myth was finally smashed in November 2017, when the British Royal Society announced that DNA tests on the relics had revealed them to belong to bears that roam the Himalayas.

THE MYTH

The word "ye" meant "the."

THE TRUTH

The word "the" was never pronounced or spelled "ye" in Old or Middle English. In Old English, the runic letter "thorn" (þ) represented the sound "th." This looked a bit like the letter "y" in handwritten scripts. Medieval printing presses did not have the letter thorn, so they used "y" instead. The "y" stuck, like a thorn in the side of subsequent writers. Today the "olde" spellings are just amusing word play, because, sadly, there would never have been a "ye olde shoppe" in "ye olde world."

***Star Trek*'s Captain Kirk did not say, "Beam me up, Scotty."** At no time in the *Star Trek* TV series or films did Captain Kirk ever say the now-immortal line. The nearest actual line within the scripts was: "Beam us up, Mr. Scott."

Brown eggs are not better for you than white eggs. This is an old wives' tale, because there is no nutritional difference between the two types of egg. The color of the shell is simply determined by the hue of the chicken that laid the egg.

Bombay Duck is not a duck. It is in fact a bottom-dwelling lizard fish, most popularly eaten in India and Bangladesh. Also known as a "bummalo," it is usually served dry, having been fried until it is so crispy it can even be crumbled over a curry.

You are probably more than 6 feet away from a rat. The adage that you are never more than 6 feet from a rat may derive from the commonly held belief that there are more rats than humans on earth. However, recent research suggests that even in New York City, a city Animal Planet referred to as "The Worst Rat City in the World," humans could possibly outnumber rats 4 to 1. For the myth to be true, it would also require rats to space themselves out evenly across the land, which has evidently never been the case.

Earwigs will not crawl into your ears. Children are commonly told by cruel adults that earwigs will crawl into their ears while they sleep and lay eggs inside their brain—an utterly terrifying thought. But, although this insect is nocturnal, it spends its nights feeding on insects and plants.

THE MYTH

Jerusalem artichokes come from Jerusalem.

THE TRUTH

The Jerusalem artichoke is a lumpy, brown-skinned vegetable, but its name is a double lie. It is not actually an artichoke, but a species of sunflower with an edible tuber, which is eaten as a root vegetable. And nor does it come from Jerusalem; the name is instead derived from *girasole*, the Italian word for sunflower, which somehow managed to get changed to "Jerusalem" along the way.

It is known by a variety of other interesting names, including sunroot, sunchoke, earth apple, or Canadian truffle. If you want to appear really clever, you can also call it a *topinambour*, a name that reportedly results from a visit by a Brazilian tribe, the Tupinambá, to the Vatican at a time when some Jerusalem artichokes were on display there. Jerusalem artichokes have a nutty flavor that appeals to many people, but be warned—they also have a reputation for causing flatulence!

31

Caesarean operations are not named after Julius Caesar.
The operation pre-dates Caesar and can be traced back to the Persian hero Rostam, who is said to have been the first person to be delivered by this now common method.

An elk is not always a moose. There is a lot of confusion between an elk and a moose. What is known as a moose in North America is known as an elk in Europe. An elk in North America, however,  belongs to a different deer family altogether, the wapiti, which do not inhabit the continent of Europe—which is just as well, because the Europeans would have to find a new name for it. Perhaps they would call it a moose?

A buffalo is not always a buffalo. A North American "buffalo" is actually a bison. Early American settlers called bison "buffalo" because that's what they looked like to them, and the name just stuck. The "American buffalo," or bison, lives only in North America, whereas "real buffalos" live only in Asia and Africa. They include the water buffalos of Asia and the Cape buffalos of sub-Saharan Africa.

Most body heat is not lost through the head. People, especially older people, are encouraged to wear something on their head during cold weather, but in fact only about ten percent of overall body heat is lost through the head. Wearing headgear of any description, therefore, is primarily a matter of personal preference or fashion.

Britain's Alan Turing did not crack the Enigma codes on his own. During World War Two, huge amounts of time and effort were employed to crack the communication codes used by the Germans on their Enigma machines. Many people of different nationalities were engaged in the task, including a group of Polish codebreakers. Alan Turing was only able to crack the codes by building on knowledge passed on by Polish mathematicians, who have gone largely uncredited in the history books.

THE MYTH

A cow started the Great Chicago Fire of 1871.

THE TRUTH

According to popular lore, a cow owned by Cate O'Leary accidentally kicked over a lantern while being milked in a barn, which then went up in flames. The fire spread quickly over three square miles of the city of Chicago, with hundreds of people killed and some 17,000 buildings destroyed. It made a good story and O'Leary—a poor Irish Catholic immigrant—made the perfect scapegoat. The story prevailed even after the journalist who started the rumor, Michael Ahern, admitted he had fabricated it. The old newspaper adage that you should never let the truth spoil a good story was never truer.

Fortune cookies did not originate in China. They are often served at the end of a meal in Chinese restaurants, but they most likely originated in Japan.

Eating bread crusts does not make your hair curl. Because curly hair was once taken to be a sign of good health, many children have been persuaded over the years that eating crusts will make their hair curl, whether they wanted curly hair or not. However, there is nothing scientific to support this advice.

Elephants do not drink through their trunks. The many uses of an elephant's dangling appendage include breathing, smelling, touching, and trumpeting. It is also used to suck up water and then squirt that water into its mouth, but it cannot, as many people suppose, drink directly through its trunk.

Humans did not evolve from monkeys or any other primate living today. This myth was supposedly perpetrated by religious zealots in the nineteenth century to discredit Darwin's theory of evolution and it remains prevalent to this day. The fact that we share a common ape ancestor (which lived up to nine million years ago) with chimpanzees is probably the cause of the misconception.

Your brain does not strictly use different sides for different activities. While it's true that many functions predominantly work either the left or right hemisphere of the brain, most of them, including reasoning, memory, and motor control, activate both sides. It has even been shown that when parts of the brain have been damaged, the lost functions can be recovered elsewhere, including within the other hemisphere.

THE MYTH

All dinosaurs were wiped out by one huge extinction event.

THE TRUTH

The Cretaceous–Paleogene extinction event that occurred approximately 66 million years ago, thought to have been caused by a massive comet or asteroid hitting the earth (possibly in what is now Mexico), *did* wipe out a huge amount of life on earth, but not all of it. Estimates put the figure at up to 75 percent of all species living on the planet at the time being permanently lost, but many avian dinosaurs (theropods) survived. The latter eventually evolved into the birds we now know and love, so in a way we live surrounded by dinosaurs to this day.

Bats are not blind. The fact that most bats hunt in the dark and use a sonar system known as "echolocation" to maneuver and find prey has led to the general assumption that bats are blind. In fact, bats can see almost as well as humans, but their sophisticated "hearing" is more useful to them than their vision.

Danish pastries do not come from Denmark. It is natural to assume that the delicious, buttery puff pastry delicacies known as Danish pastries originated in Denmark. In fact, they were originally Austrian, being brought from Austria to Denmark in the nineteenth century. They are still known in Denmark as "Viennese bread."

A mother bird will not reject a baby bird you've picked up. Birds have a very limited sense of smell, so they will not abandon a baby just because it has been handled by a human, but you should still avoid disturbing wildlife regardless!

Eating chocolate does not cause acne. Cruel parents often tell their children that eating chocolate causes acne, but that is probably a crafty ploy to keep all the chocolate to themselves, as there is no evidence whatsoever to support the claim. Good news for those of us with a sweet tooth.

You do not use only ten percent of your brain. An oft-quoted faux fact is that you never use more than ten percent of your brain, but actually most of your brain is active all of the time, and all areas of your brain are required to perform important functions. There are various possible origins of this myth, and they all derive from misunderstandings about the incredibly complex nature of the human brain.

THE MYTH

Joan of Arc was burned as a witch.

THE TRUTH

Joan of Arc (Jeanne d'Arc), nicknamed "The Maid of Orléans," was a French national heroine. At the tender age of 18, she led the French army to victories over the English. On May 30, 1431, she was burned at the stake, not for sorcery, but for heresy, because she dressed as a man.

December 25 was not the birthday of Jesus Christ. Christians celebrate December 25 as the birthday of Jesus Christ, but there is no evidence that he was born on that day. It was Pope Julius I, around 350 years after the birth of Christ, who decreed that it should be celebrated on the random date of December 25.

Xmas is not an abbreviation. When Christmas is written as Xmas, it is not an abbreviation, as some people believe, and there's no truth in the assertion, therefore, that it's a ruse to take "Christ" out of "Christmas." The X, in fact, derives from the Greek letter *chi*, which is often used in the Greek language as an abbreviation of "Christ."

Hair does not grow after death. If, as some people believe, hair continues to grow after death, it would not take long for a buried corpse to become positively hirsute. In the days following death, skin tissue recedes as it loses moisture, which can give the impression that the hair has grown a little, but it hasn't.

Bagpipes did not originate in Scotland. Go almost anywhere in Scotland and sooner or later you will hear the distinctive sound of the bagpipes. Because the instrument is such an important part of the nation's culture, it is perfectly natural to assume that 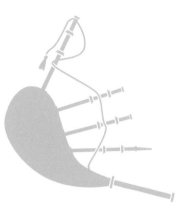 bagpipes originated there. There are, however, records of bagpipes in existence all over Europe and parts of Asia for over 2,000 years, whereas the first record of bagpipes being heard in Scotland appeared in 1547.

Humans do not have only five senses. The main senses attributed to humans are sight, hearing, smell, taste, and touch. But we have more sense than that, at least according to the scientists who include other stimuli recognized by the central nervous system as "senses." Some say that we have at least nine specific senses, others that we have as many as 21. Our additional senses apparently include a sense of space, balance, temperature, pain, vibration, hunger, thirst, and even time. I hope that makes sense.

THE MYTH

Marie Antoinette said, "Let them eat cake."

THE TRUTH

The phrase was first recorded in the autobiography of French writer Jean-Jacques Rousseau in 1765, when Marie Antoinette was just nine years old, and it actually translates as "Let them eat brioches," so the widely believed claim is wrong on two counts. The phrase was later attributed to Marie Antoinette by her enemies, who wanted to consolidate her reputation as hard-hearted and disconnected from her subjects.

Not all dogs bark. "Barking" is traditionally the answer to the question "What noise do dogs make?" But the answer is not wholly accurate, for there are many breeds that do not bark. One of those is the Basenji, a hunting dog that originated in central Africa, which produces a strange yodeling sound.

Salt does not remove beet stains. A commonly accepted way to remove a beet stain is to pour salt on it. Do not do this, as the salt merely sets the stain and makes it almost impossible to remove. It is more effective to hold a sponge soaked in cold water on it, then blot it with a dry cloth. Or, better still, just be more careful what you do with your beets!

Peanuts are not nuts. Also known as a groundnut or a goober, the peanut is actually a legume, an edible seed in a pod, like beans and peas. Nuts grow on trees, but peanuts grow underground.

Cracking your knuckles does not cause arthritis. Many people believe that cracking your knuckles (or the joints in your neck, back, or toes) causes arthritis, but scientific investigations have found no evidence that this is the case. Some people wince when someone nearby causes their knuckles to make that horrible cracking noise, but you can reassure them it's just small bubbles of fluid in the synovial joints popping—and it's perfectly harmless.

Marco Polo didn't bring pasta to Italy from China. The Venetian merchant and explorer Marco Polo, who traveled extensively throughout China in the fourteenth century, is often associated with the introduction of pasta to Italy. In fact, records show pasta being made in Italy long before Polo embarked upon his epic travels to the Far East.

THE MYTH

Chewing gum takes seven years to digest.

THE TRUTH

It is true that chewing gum is indigestible, but you do not have to wait seven years for it to go through your system. Your digestive tract will deal with it soon enough and pass it through when you go to the bathroom. It is, however, preferable to discard it yourself rather than swallow it, just in case it gets stuck in your throat (but please don't discard it on the ground, or on a wall, or under a desk, because that's just rude). This is one myth that could stick around for some time to come, though, which might very well give you something to chew on.

A goldfish's memory is not short. The memory of a goldfish can be counted in months, not just three seconds, as is often claimed. Scientific experiments have shown that a goldfish's memory can generally retain information for up to three, and sometimes even five, months.

Albert Einstein did not fail a mathematics exam. It is often said that the great scientist Albert Einstein once failed a math exam. But the facts do not add up—he was brilliant at arithmetic and got consistently good marks in school. He did fail a school entrance exam, but that was set in French and his first language was German.

The Buddha (Siddhartha Gautama) was not obese. The laughing, chubby Buddha image we are so familiar with is actually a representation of the tenth-century Chinese folklore deity, Budhai. It is more likely, given his ascetic lifestyle, that Siddhartha Gautama (who taught in Ancient India around the fourth century BCE) was quite lean.

 **The forbidden fruit was probably not an apple.** According to the Book of Genesis, the forbidden fruit of knowledge of good and evil was eaten by Adam and Eve in the Garden of Eden against God's advice. In the interests of modesty, the fruit is usually depicted as an apple, being considered a typical fruit that may have grown in a garden at that time. Scholars have since suggested that fruits grown back then were more likely to be grapes, figs, apricots, or etrogs (a citrus fruit).

There may have been more than three wise men. Tradition has it that three wise men (or Magi) traveled to Bethlehem to pay homage to the Baby Jesus. The number of wise men seems to have derived from the three gifts of gold, frankincense, and myrrh mentioned in the New Testament, but the number of wise men is not given. It is likely that there were many more, because news of the birth of Jesus would probably have spread like wildfire.

THE MYTH

People in the Middle Ages generally died at a very early age.

THE TRUTH

People in the Middle Ages did not always expect to die as young as you might suppose. One figure often cited as the average life expectancy in the Middle Ages is "thirty-something," but that figure was greatly influenced by a high infant mortality rate. Those who made it to adulthood in medieval England, particularly those who enjoyed the privileges and diet of the upper classes, could expect to live to a healthy 50 or 60, and some lived even longer.

The brothers Grimm did not invent Grimms' Fairy Tales.
In the nineteenth century, Jacob and Wilhelm Grimm collected, edited, and published existing fairy tales which had previously only been passed down orally, but they did not create them.

. . . .

Dinosaurs were not all carnivores. While there is evidence that some dinosaurs, including Tyrannosaurus rex and velociraptors, did hunt and eat meat, scientists also know from fossilized teeth and dung that most dinosaurs were in fact vegetarian.

. . . .

You don't hear the sea when you hold a seashell to your ear. Sorry to disappoint, but the sound you hear is really the sound of your immediate surroundings resonating inside the seashell. You can get the same effect with an ordinary cup that has been nowhere near the sea.

Schizophrenia is not multiple personality disorder. The proper term for the disorder in which one person experiences two or more distinct identities, or personality states, is Dissociative Identity Disorder. Schizophrenia refers to an altogether separate and complex mental disorder, characterized by difficulty in understanding reality and consequent abnormal social behavior. The confusion comes in part from an old, looser definition of the term "schizophrenia," and in part from the literal translation of the term, which comes from the Greek words for "to split" and "mind"—but this was intended to refer to the splitting of mental functions, not a split personality.

Thousand Island dressing does not come from a thousand islands. The name conjures up visions of an intrepid explorer island-hopping to find a thousand different flavors to mix together, but it is considered more likely by historians to have been made by or for the fishermen of the "Thousand Islands" area of the Upper St. Lawrence River between the US and Canada. Various local residents have been cited as the inventor of the dressing, so who you choose to believe depends on which islanders you talk to on which island.

THE MYTH

The Salem Witches were burned at the stake.

THE TRUTH

Those found guilty at the Salem Witch Trials in Massachusetts in the seventeenth century were not burned at the stake. Five died in prison, including two infant children, 19 were hanged, and one, an old man, was pressed to death under heavy stones. The common misconception that witches were always burned at the stake probably comes from Europe's proclivity for death by fire at that time, and for incinerating the bodies of those accused of witchcraft to prevent them from performing their black magic from beyond the grave.

Within ten years of the executions, it was ruled that the trials had been a mistake. Within 20 years, the families of those convicted had received compensation.

Centipedes do not have 100 legs. Centipede comes from the Latin "centi" (100) and "pedes" (feet). In fact, each centipede has a random number of legs. Some have as many as 354, others as few as 30.

The longest bone in the human body is not the backbone. The backbone is not just one bone, but a series of interlocking bones known as vertebrae. The longest bone is actually the thighbone, or femur, which is on average just under 27 percent of a person's height.

Lead pencils do not contain lead. "Black lead pencils" have always contained non-toxic graphite, mixed with a clay binder, but they have never contained lead. When graphite was discovered in the 1500s, it was mistaken for lead, and by the time the error was discovered, the name "lead pencil" had stuck.

Henry Morton Stanley did not say, "Dr. Livingstone, I presume?" This is the quotation attributed to the explorer Henry Morton Stanley when he found the missing missionary, David Livingstone, in Africa. However, it is now believed to be a complete fabrication on Stanley's part, because he later tore out the diary page he wrote it on, and Livingstone made no mention of it in his own account of the famous 1871 meeting.

You do not have to invent a trick to join The Magic Circle. The Magic Circle is the leading society for magicians in the UK. To join as an associate requires a proven interest in conjuring and to join as a member requires some knowledge or experience of magic, so it is not necessary to invent a trick to be accepted into the fold.

THE MYTH

King John signed the Magna Carta.

THE TRUTH

King John didn't actually "sign" his approval of the Magna Carta at Runnymede on June 15, 1215. Instead, he allowed a court official (called a "spigurnel") to apply the Great Seal of the Realm on his behalf. The purpose of the *Magna Carta Libertatum,* or "Great Charter of the Liberties," was to set out the laws of the land and to limit the power of the king. It is also commonly assumed that, once signed, the Magna Carta entered immediately into common law, but within months the document had been annulled by the Pope and the treaty broken on both sides. It wasn't until 1297 that Edward I agreed to the version which eventually entered the statute book.

Napoleon Bonaparte was not as short as most people think. Napoleon's height is considered by many historians to have been around 5 feet 7 inches, which wasn't exactly tall, but was taller than the average Frenchman in his time. His nickname, *Le Petit Caporal* ("The Little Corporal"), was probably a term of affection that stemmed from the camaraderie he enjoyed with his men.

Thomas Crapper did not invent the flushing toilet. Crapper, a respected plumber and manufacturer of bathroom ware, did market an improved flush system developed by one of his employees, the inventor Albert Giblin, but several versions of a flush toilet pre-dated the one they produced. So that's another misconception that's gone down the toilet.

The first powered airplane flight was not made by the Wright brothers in 1903. Although the brothers have generally received the credit, there is evidence that other pioneers had achieved some form of flight before them. They include Clément Ader in 1890, Gustave Whitehead in 1901, and Richard Pearse in 1903.

James Watt did not invent the steam engine. It is popularly believed that the Scottish engineer James Watt invented the steam engine in 1781, after watching a kettle boil

and seeing the steam force the lid to rise. In fact, he actually made improvements to Thomas Newcomen's 1712 steam engine, and the kettle story is a load of hot air.

Piles are not caused by sitting on cold surfaces. There is no medical truth to the old wives' tale that sitting on a cold surface can cause piles. Piles (hemorrhoids) are swollen blood vessels in the rectum and anus, caused primarily by straining in the attempt to empty one's bowels. Very often, people do not know they have them, but they can become very painful and even cause bleeding. Foods that help keep stools regular and sufficiently soft, such as fruit and vegetables, help you avoid constipation and therefore help prevent the condition.

THE MYTH

Waking a sleepwalker is dangerous.

THE TRUTH

People are often advised that waking a sleepwalker is dangerous, but there is no proof that doing so gives the sleepwalker a shock or even, as some believe, a heart attack. However, it is still best not to wake them suddenly, just in case they hurt themselves by coming out of their very deep, non-REM sleep too quickly (they might bump into something or fall down some stairs in their disoriented state). Instead, you should gently lead the slumbering person back to bed, where there is much less chance of them causing themselves harm.

Slaves did not build the pyramids. There is recent archaeological evidence that the pyramid builders of Ancient Egypt were not slaves, but Egyptian laborers who were well paid to do the work. Laborers who died on the job are now known to have been buried within the pyramids, an honor that would never have been bestowed on slaves.

. . . .

You don't need to wait to swim after eating. In spite of dire warnings to the contrary, swimming right after eating is perfectly safe—provided you don't overdo it (a four-course meal right before any form of strenuous exercise is not recommended if you want that four-course meal to stay where it is).

. . . .

Toads will not give you warts. Toads have a bumpy skin which in some species secretes a poisonous milky substance. This can cause some irritation to human skin, but certainly not warts (which are caused only by viruses). So, don't worry—handling a toad will not cause you to croak.

A black belt is not the top-level belt. In martial arts, a black belt does not always denote the top skill level, or "master" status. The black belt introduced by Kanō Jigorō, the founder of judo, simply indicates competency in the basic techniques and principles, and can be achieved in as little as three years.

Bulls are not enraged by the color red. A bull's vision does not even register red as a particularly bright color. They actually charge as a reaction to the general threat of the matador, so the color of the matador's cape is incidental. So, showing a red rag to a bull is not dangerous, unless you go out of your way to provoke it at the same time!

THE MYTH

There was mass hysteria after the radio dramatization of _The War of the Worlds_, because people thoughts Martians had actually invaded earth.

THE TRUTH

This myth is actually a misconception about a misconception. It is widely believed that Orson Welles caused panic with his 1938 radio dramatization of H. G. Wells's _The War of the Worlds_. Convinced that the world had been invaded by Martians, the American people reportedly fled from their homes as mass hysteria swept through the country. But the truth of the matter is that not many people even listened to the show, and the only stories of panic were those invented by newspapers for the editions they printed the next day.

Nero did not fiddle while Rome burned.
It's a great story, but, according to the historian
Tacitus, the emperor Nero was not even in Rome
at the time of the Great Fire in 64 AD (though
he did return upon hearing the news). Later
paintings depict Nero playing a fiddle, but the
instrument hadn't even been invented, which
makes the original myth doubly mythical.

**Chastity belts weren't used to stop wives from straying
while their husbands went off to fight.** A belief that
prevails to this day is that the chastity belt was used on
ladies at court while their knights in shining armor went
off to fight the Crusades in the Holy Land. In fact, chastity
belts were very rare and not very practical or sanitary
over a long period of time.

**Sherlock Holmes never said, "Elementary, my dear
Watson."** Scour the books written by Arthur Conan Doyle
and you will not find this expression anywhere. The nearest
he came to it (in three different stories) was: "Exactly, my
dear Watson."

Shaving does not cause hair to grow thicker. Hair which has never been cut has a tapered end, whereas the act of cutting or shaving leaves a blunt and therefore wider hair end. Because of this, cut hair *appears* coarser, and therefore darker, due to its sharper, unworn edges, but the act of cutting hair does not affect its growth in any way.

S O S does not stand for "Save Our Souls" or "Save Our Ship." In fact, the Morse code distress signal • • • - - - • • • (dot dot dot, dash dash dash, dot dot dot) does not mean anything at all. It was originally introduced as a generic distress signal in Germany, simply because of its easy-to-transmit sequence. The letters "S O S" happen to use the same symbols in Morse code. Sorry to dash your hopes!

THE MYTH

The Iron Maiden was a form of torture.

THE TRUTH

The most bloodthirsty torture device of the Middle Ages was the Iron Maiden, right? Wrong. The upright coffin-shaped box with numerous spikes that supposedly impaled anyone unfortunate enough to be shut inside was just a nineteenth-century joke. Many examples were made in the 1800s and put on display at fair sideshows and in museums, but this decidedly gory way of creating a human pin cushion was never actually used.

You shouldn't tilt your head back to stop a nosebleed.
If you do, you will likely swallow your own blood, which
is unpleasant. You should, instead, lean forward slightly
to allow the blood to flow out. If you pinch your nostrils
together at the same time, it will encourage natural clotting.

**Urine does not soothe a jellyfish
sting.** You can pee on a jellyfish sting
as much as you like (whatever turns
you on), but it doesn't soothe the sting
and it may even cause it to burn more than
it already does. Vinegar, on the other hand, works on
many jellyfish stings, so always take a bottle of vinegar
to the beach just in case.

Excessive sugar does not make kids hyperactive. Many
parents use the simple solution of withdrawing sweet
things to keep their kids calm, but there is no medical
evidence that it will make the slightest bit of difference.

Oranges are not called oranges because they are orange. The citrus fruit has been called an "orange" since the fourteenth century, but the word came from the Sanskrit *nāranga*, meaning "fragrant." The word was not used to refer to the color orange until the early 1500s. Until that point, the color we now refer to as orange was called "yellow-red," or ġeolurēad.

You don't swallow spiders in your sleep. There's a widespread belief that we each swallow an average of seven spiders a year—apparently, they crawl into your open mouth while you snooze. But even if, for some bizarre reason known only to the spider, it did want to crawl down your throat, it would be deterred from doing so by all the scary noises, movements, and vibrations that come from a sleeping person's body.

THE MYTH

Duck quacks don't echo.

THE TRUTH

If you go up a mountain or stand in a tunnel and shout, you will hear an echo of your own voice coming back to you, in common with the sounds made by any creature from the animal kingdom. Except duck quacks, according to accepted wisdom. Scientists, however, have more recently proven in echo chambers that there is in fact an echo from a duck quack. The myth arose from the fact that the echo of a duck quack is simply too weak for us to hear it. You could, of course, try your own experiment by taking your duck to your local canyon—but you might be thought quackers if you did.

Specific areas of the tongue do not detect different tastes. Many of us learned this myth at school, but the truth is that, although different areas of the tongue are more sensitive to particular tastes, all sensations of taste come from all areas of the tongue.

Tarzan did not say, "Me Tarzan, you Jane." This phrase is usually attributed to Tarzan (played by Johnny Weissmuller) in the 1932 film *Tarzan the Ape Man*. But he never said it. The nearest he got was: "Jane, Tarzan. Jane, Tarzan."

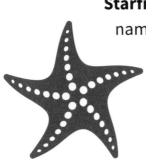

Starfish are not fish. In spite of their name, starfish are, technically speaking, star-shaped echinoderms with five or more "arms" radiating from a central disc. Now you know!

Pope Joan did not reign as the world's first female Pope. It was widely believed for centuries that Pope Joan reigned from 855 to 857, after disguising herself as a man in order to enter the Church in the first place. Unfortunately, there is no real evidence to support the claim, because the Pope from 847 to 855 was Leo IV, and he was succeeded by Benedict III, from 855 to 888. If there had been a female Pope, it would surely have caused a sensation and the paparazzi of the day would have been on the story like a shot.

Crispy seaweed does not come from the sea. Crispy seaweed is a dish served in many Chinese restaurants, but many of us have been surprised to discover that it does not taste of the sea. That is because it is not seaweed at all, but cabbage! The cabbage, usually pak choi or kale, is cooked in a hot wok and then seasoned with salt, sugar, and five-spice powder. Delicious!

THE MYTH

March hares are mad.

THE TRUTH

Hares do indulge in strange and excitable behavior, including pseudo-boxing and jumping for no apparent reason, during their breeding season, which happens to fall over the month of March in Europe. Much of their strange behavior, however, is part of the ritual to determine male supremacy during the mating season, and the boxing we see is often a female's attempt to ward off a courting male. The expression "mad as a March hare" is nowadays used to describe any animal that displays unpredictable behavior, or any human being who doesn't quite stick to the social norms of the day.

Cromwell did not say, "Paint me, warts and all." This was supposedly said by Oliver Cromwell when his portrait was being painted by Sir Peter Lely, because he did not want to be flattered in the manner of the king he had executed, Charles I. Unfortunately there is no evidence that he spoke those exact words, though it's a great-sounding phrase.

French fries are not French. French fries were first cooked up in Belgium, where they remain as popular as ever as *frites*. People in the UK call them "chips," which is in turn the American term for what the British know as crisps. Why must life be so confusing?

Jimmy Cagney never said, "You dirty rat." This is a favorite phrase of impersonators doing film star James Cagney, but the words he actually said were: "Come out and take it, you dirty, yellow-bellied rat."

Isaac Newton was not hit on the head by an apple. It is often said that an apple falling out of a tree onto his head caused the great British scientist, Isaac Newton, to formulate his theory of gravity. The tree itself remains standing in the orchard at Woolsthorpe Manor, near

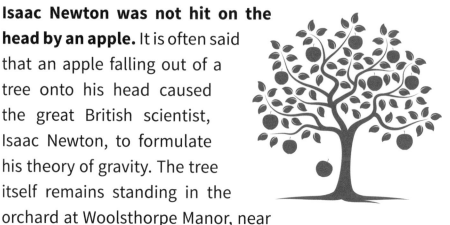

Grantham. Newton's own account did refer to apples falling to the ground, but he said nothing about an apple hitting him on the head, so the "core" of the story at least is a myth.

A coin dropped from a skyscraper will not kill anyone it hits at the bottom. The well-known myth usually associated with the dropping of a penny from the top of the Empire State Building in New York has been disproven by scientists. In fact, a falling coin will tumble on its way down, a bit like a leaf does, so it does not gain enough momentum to hurt anyone on the ground. A bag of coins, however, would be a completely different ballgame!

THE MYTH

The United States Declaration of Independence was passed on the fourth of July.

THE TRUTH

The Declaration of Independence was, in fact, formally passed on the second of July, not the fourth. John Adams, the first Vice President of the United States (and the second President) even stated at the time: "The Second Day of July 1776 will be the most memorable Epocha in the History of America." So why then do Americans celebrate on the fourth of July? Because that was the day that the Second Continental Congress approved and adopted the wording at the Pennsylvania State House, now known as Independence Hall.

The Swiss roll is not Swiss. The sponge cake filled with whipped cream, jam, or icing is generally believed to have come from Austria, not Switzerland. Americans know it as "jelly roll," so we don't have to worry about where it originated.

Blood is never blue. Some people believe that blood is sometimes blue, because veins appear through the skin as blue, but this is only caused by the penetration of light through the skin. Human blood is always red, wherever it flows, including in the veins.

The Canary Islands have no connection with canaries. The name probably comes from the Latin name *Canariae Insulae*, meaning "Islands of the Dogs." And, just to confuse matters further, the "dogs" were probably not dogs, but seals, because the Latin for the seals that inhabited that area was *canis marinus* (sea dog).

Ferdinand Magellan was not the first explorer to circumnavigate the world.  The Portuguese explorer would have been first if he'd completed the journey, but he was killed in battle after taking spears in the leg, arm, neck, and face 16 months before the expedition returned home. Eighteen surviving crew members under Magellan's successor, Juan Sebastian Elcano, did go on to earn the honor of being the first people to circumnavigate the world in a single expedition.

The "hair of the dog" is not the best hangover cure. Many people who have drunk too much alcohol and suffer with a hangover the following morning believe that the best cure for it is the hair of the dog that bit you—in other words, another alcoholic drink. Unfortunately, though it may stave off the effects of the hangover for a while, it cures nothing—in fact, it prolongs the hangover until you've recovered from the hair of the dog!

THE MYTH

Christopher Columbus discovered America.

THE TRUTH

Everyone knows that Columbus discovered America after sailing westward from Portugal in 1492 in the hope of finding a new route to the East Indies. Except he didn't. Indigenous peoples had been living in what we now call America for around 20,000 years before Columbus arrived, and some Vikings had also "discovered" it around 1000 AD. Columbus didn't even reach the mainland of the American continent, because he landed instead on various Caribbean islands. In later expeditions, he "discovered" yet more Caribbean islands and set foot on the Caribbean coastlines of Central and South America, but he never set foot on the mainland of North America.

Mozart did not write "Twinkle, Twinkle, Little Star" when he was five. The lullaby was in fact written by English poet Jane Taylor much later, in 1806, but Mozart did compose variations set to the same old French melody it was written to (the same one that is still used for "Baa, Baa, Black Sheep").

The Hundred Years' War did not last a hundred years. The Hundred Years' War was a series of conflicts, not one continuous war, fought between England and France over the succession to the French throne. Furthermore, it lasted from 1337 to 1453: a grand total of 116 years.

Alexander Graham Bell did not invent the telephone. In 1876, Bell registered a patent for the practical telephone he had invented, but a more rudimentary version had been invented by the Italian Antonio Meucci 16 years  previously. Meucci sued Bell and initiated fraud charges against him, but he died before a verdict could be reached, leaving Bell forever more as the "official" inventor of the telephone, whatever the rights and wrongs of the patents that were registered.

Bananas don't grow on trees. To most people, the banana is a fruit that grows on trees. According to botanists, however, banana plants are  classed as herbaceous and the banana itself is technically a berry. This is because true tree stems contain woody tissue, which the stems of a banana plant do not, so bananas actually grow on herbaceous plants. It's enough to make you "go bananas."

Elephants do not go to a graveyard to die. According to legend, an elephant breaks away from the herd as it approaches the end of its life and travels to a "graveyard" that contains the bones of its ancestors. This myth has been popularized in several films, and certainly the bones of dead elephants have occasionally been found together, but the idea of whole "graveyards" remains very much a "bone" of contention.

THE MYTH

Lobsters scream when boiled.

THE TRUTH

Many people will tell you that lobsters scream when boiled, but the truth is that lobsters are incapable of screaming as they have no vocal cords. The noise they sometimes make when placed in boiling water is caused by air bubbles trapped in the shell finding their way out. So they're definitely not screaming in agony, although the matter of whether lobsters feel pain or not remains open to debate and is the subject of ongoing scientific research. Switzerland is leading the humanitarian way by banning cooks from boiling lobsters alive—just in case.

Pluto is not the ninth planet of the solar system. Pluto was considered to be the ninth planet in our solar system until many other similar-sized objects were discovered in the circumstellar disc known as the Kuiper belt. Since 2006, when the definition of what constitutes a planet was changed, Pluto has been reclassified as a dwarf planet.

The sun is white. Though we nearly always see it as either yellow, orange, or red, this is only due to its short-wavelength colors (green, blue, and violet) being filtered out through our atmosphere. Seen from space, the sun shows its true colors—that is, all of its colors mixed together, which to our eyes appears more white than anything.

There is no corn in corned beef. That corn is used as an ingredient within corned beef is a fallacy. The "corn" referred to is actually large grains (or "corns") of salt, which are used to form a brine in which the beef is soaked.

Bunsen did not invent the Bunsen burner. The Bunsen burner used in laboratories is named after the German chemist Robert Bunsen, but he simply redesigned earlier models of gas burners, including one designed by Michael Faraday. Much of the development of the Bunsen burner was carried out by Bunsen's largely forgotten assistant Peter Desaga, whose contribution, therefore, appears to have gone up in flames.

Hoover did not invent the vacuum cleaner. The domestic vacuum cleaner is often called a "hoover," after its so-called "inventor" William Henry Hoover. But credit for the invention should not go to Hoover; it should go to Hubert Cecil Booth and David T. Kenney, who independently invented powered suction cleaners in 1901. Booth's invention worked well enough, but it had to be pulled by a horse and it needed six people to operate it! In 1908, Hoover bought the patent for the first upright vacuum cleaner from another designer, James Murray Spangler, and set up the Hoover Company we know today—but it was never his invention.

THE MYTH

Henry VIII wrote "Greensleeves."

THE TRUTH

It is generally believed that King Henry VIII of England wrote the song "Greensleeves" for his lover Anne Boleyn (before he married her), but in reality he was far too busy being king to have any time for such frippery. There is no proof he wrote the song, which was first published as "A Newe Northern Dittye of ye Ladye Green Sleves" in 1580, more than 30 years after the king's death.

Diamonds are not formed from compressed coal. Diamonds and coal are different forms of carbon. The carbon that forms diamonds is millions of years older and a different formation to the carbon that becomes coal. Blame the perpetuation of the myth on the comic book hero Superman, who turned a lump of coal into a perfect diamond just by squeezing it in his hand.

Marinating meat for a long period is unnecessary. Cooks often advocate marinating meat for hours on end, but marinade only penetrates meat to a depth of a few millimeters, a process which takes an hour or so. Marinating for longer than an hour is generally unnecessary and if you leave it for more than four hours it can start to spoil the food.

You should not store eggs in the fridge door. Fridges often have a holder in the door to store eggs, but it's actually the worst place to keep them. Because the temperature is changed every time the fridge door is opened, eggs are less likely to go bad if maintained at a more constant temperature at the back of the fridge.

King Harold may not have been killed by an arrow to his eye. The only evidence that he was is an image on the Bayeux Tapestry. Some scholars, however, argue that Harold is actually the soldier falling to the ground and being trampled by horses to the right of the famous "arrow-in-eye" figure, which is more in keeping with an earlier description of the battle. Other scholars argue that the Bayeux Tapestry depicts two wounds in order, such that Harold first received an arrow to the eye and was then mutilated in the ensuing cavalry charge. That view is strengthened by the fact that the inscription *"Harold Rex Interfectus Est"* ("King Harold is killed") runs the length of both images. Either way, it was probably not the most pleasant of deaths.

Sardines are not a breed of fish. Sardines are fish, it's true, but there is in fact no such fish as a sardine. It is, instead, the generic term for many small oily fish of the herring family, as is the term "pilchard," which is pretty much the same thing as a "sardine." The name "sardine" is believed to have derived from the island of Sardinia, where these small fish were once plentiful.

THE MYTH

John F. Kennedy inadvertently said "I am a jam doughnut" in German, instead of "I am a Berliner."

THE TRUTH

The Cold War speech made by JFK in West Berlin in 1963 is widely considered one of his best speeches, and he even used the phrase "*Ich bin ein Berliner*" correctly (because he was actually saying "I am one with the people of Berlin," not "I come from Berlin"). The legend that the phrase changed meaning by leaving in the indefinite article "*ein*," and that the crowd laughed at his hilarious error is a total fallacy—the crowd of Berliners present actually applauded the sentiment and only laughed at the president's intentional jokes. The word "*Berliner*" *is* used in some parts of Germany to refer to a jam doughnut, but not in Berlin itself. If he had said "*Ich bin ein Berliner Pfannkuchen*," it would have been a different matter altogether.

Alexander Fleming did not discover penicillin. Although Fleming is widely thought to have discovered penicillin in 1928, it was actually discovered 32 years earlier by a French medical student, Ernest Duchesne, but he didn't recognize its potential benefits at the time. Fleming was, however, first to discover the antibiotic properties of penicillin.

Thomas Edison did not invent the incandescent light bulb. British inventor Joseph Swan deserves the credit for developing the first practical light bulb, having successfully demonstrated one in operation in January 1879, nine months ahead of Edison's first successful demonstration on the other side of the Atlantic.

Bread and milk are not good for hedgehogs. Although these creatures enjoy bread and milk, they will have tummy problems after eating. If you want to leave a meal out for a visiting hedgehog, use meaty pet food and water instead.

Everest is not the world's tallest mountain. Mount Everest in the Himalayas is usually deemed to be the world's highest mountain, but that depends on how you measure a mountain. Everest is the tallest mountain above sea level, granted, but the mountain-island of Mauna Kea on Hawaii beats it when measured from the seabed, and Mount Chimborazo in Ecuador reaches further towards space than either of them, because it is situated on the earth's equatorial bulge. Like many things in life, it just depends on how you look at it.

Spaghetti does not grow on trees. A spaghetti harvest reported on the current affairs program *Panorama* in 1957 showed peasants in Switzerland gathering strands of spaghetti from a spaghetti tree. But it was, of course, a "mockumentary" rather than a documentary, since it was an April Fool's hoax pulled by the BBC.

THE MYTH

Cut an earthworm in half and it will become two.

THE TRUTH

The story goes that if you cut a worm in two, both parts will regenerate and create two whole new worms. Unfortunately, this is not the case. Although the "head" part may survive and generate a new tail if the cut did not affect its clitellum (the swollen band by its neck), the original tail cannot generate a new head and must therefore die. The myth perhaps arose from the ability of the planarium flatworm to regenerate into whole worms from even tiny segments—but these are not your ordinary garden worms.

Henry Ford did not invent the assembly line. Henry Ford is often credited with inventing the assembly line, but such a system was in use long before his time. The Venetian Arsenal shipyards and armories utilized an assembly system as far back as the twelfth century, so Ford simply finessed the idea in 1913 to build his Model T motor cars.

Cowboys did not all wear Stetsons. Cowboys in popular culture always wear Stetson hats, but in fact the bowler hat was initially the most popular headgear for cowboys in the Old West, because they were tight-fitting and less likely to blow off in the wind. The bowler hat eventually became unfashionable after the Stetson company started making much cooler hats for the Union Cavalry.

The "ten-gallon hat"—a name given to some types of braided hats worn by cowboys—does not hold ten gallons. Its name may come from the Spanish word *galón*, meaning braid, or possibly from a corruption of the Spanish phrase *tan galán*, which translates as "really handsome."

King Alfred did not burn any cakes. A popular story has it that King Alfred was asked by a peasant woman who had given him shelter to keep an eye on some wheaten cakes cooking on her grate, and that Alfred was so absorbed with his own problems (understandably so—he was on the run from the Vikings) that he forgot about them and they ended up like charcoal. It's a "grate" story, but one that didn't appear until hundreds of years later.

The clock tower at the Houses of Parliament in London is not called Big Ben. Tourists stand proudly in front of the tower to take their selfies, but what many do not realize is that "Big Ben" is just a nickname, which originally applied only to the Great Bell at the top. The tower itself, which used to be officially known as St. Stephen's Tower, is now called Queen Elizabeth Tower, renamed in 2012 to honor the Diamond Jubilee of Queen Elizabeth II.

THE MYTH

The weather on St. Swithin's Day determines the weather for the following 40 days.

THE TRUTH

The myth goes, for example, that if it rains on St. Swithin's Day (July 15 in the UK), it will continue to rain thereafter for 40 days and 40 nights. According to tradition, the eponymous saint requested that he be buried outside the Old Minster in Winchester, which was exactly what happened when he died in 862 AD. When his remains were moved inside the cathedral a hundred years later, the saint is said to have been so incensed that he caused it to rain for the next 40 days. Unsurprisingly, records show no continuous period of identical weather following St. Swithin's Day.

Beef olives do not contain olives. Unlike beef tomatoes, which are all tomato, the beef olive contains beef, but no olives. The name probably arose because the shape of each beef olive (which is essentially beef wrapped around a stuffing) does look a bit like the shape of an olive.

Magpies do not steal shiny things. The "thieving magpie" has a reputation for gathering and hoarding trinkets and the like, but although the bird is a scavenger of all manner of objects, it does not live up to its claimed attraction to jewelery. Recent research suggests the magpie may even be scared of shiny objects.

Scotch eggs did not originate in Scotland. Scotch eggs are boiled eggs wrapped in roughly minced, or "scotched," sausage meat, coated in breadcrumbs and deep fried. Their modern name, therefore, is an abbreviation of "scotched eggs," and should not be taken to imply any connection to Scotland. The London department store Fortnum & Mason claims to have invented them in 1738.

Stilton is not made in Stilton. It sounds logical that Stilton cheese should come from the English village of Stilton, but the big cheeses in the European Commission have given this blue-veined cheese Protected Geographical Indication status to ensure that it continues to be made only in the counties of Derbyshire, Leicestershire, and Nottinghamshire. The village of Stilton is in the county of Cambridgeshire, so cheese made in Stilton cannot be called Stilton, whether it was originally made there or not—there is no concrete evidence either way, so hard cheese, Stilton!

"Posh" does not mean "port out, starboard home." The word "posh" is often said to derive from the early days of passenger ships travelling from England to India, because it was more comfortable on the port side travelling to India out of the heat of the sun, with the reverse being true when sailing back home to England. This is unlikely to be true, because the story didn't actually appear until the 1930s. Some etymologists claim that the word is more likely to have derived from nineteenth-century slang for a dandy.

THE MYTH

Houdini drowned in a water tank.

THE TRUTH

Harry Houdini was a great magician and escape artist. He wriggled free from all manner of restraints, including handcuffs, jails, and even a paper bag (without tearing it). He is commonly believed to have drowned in his "Chinese Water Torture Cell" after being locked inside and immersed upside down into a large tank of water, but this was only dreamed up for the 1953 film *Houdini*, 27 years after his actual death. The cause of his real-life death was peritonitis, almost certainly caused by a series of blows to the stomach. Houdini always boasted that he could withstand such an attack, but when one of his students launched a surprise attack he was apparently "unprepared" to withstand the blows to his abdomen. His appendix ruptured and he succumbed to peritonitis several days later.

IMAGE CREDITS

If you're interested in finding out more
about our books, find us at
www.skyhorsepublishing.com.